Everything You Need to Know About

Schizophrenia

Hearing voices is one common symptom of schizophrenia.

Everything
You Need to
Know About

Schizophrenia

Michelle S. Friedman

Rosen Publishing Group, Inc.
New York

To Mom and Andrew, for loving and supporting me unconditionally, and to the individuals and families living with schizophrenia who have enriched the lives of others by sharing their experiences.

Published in 2000 by The Rosen Publishing Group, Inc.
29 East 21st Street, New York, NY 10010

Library of Congress Cataloging-in-Publication Data

Friedman, Michelle S.
    Everything you need to know about schizophrenia / Michelle S. Friedman.
        p. cm. — (The need to know library)
    Includes bibliographical references and index.
    Summary: Discusses schizophrenia, its diagnosis and treatment, early warning signs, and how it can affect a teen's life.
    ISBN 0-8239-3091-2 (lib. bdg.)
    1. Schizophrenia—Juvenile literature. [1. Schizophrenia. 2. Mental illness.] I. Title. II. Series.
RC514.F74 1999
616.89'82 21—dc21
                                                              99-042592

Manufactured in the United States of America

Contents

It can be hard to deal with a loved one suffering from schizophrenia.

Introduction

Debra had made honor roll every year since ninth grade. However, in her senior year of high school, everything changed. She began to notice that the food she ate tasted funny, and she started to suspect that she was being poisoned by aliens. She stopped eating. Within four weeks, she had lost nearly thirty pounds. She also began to hear voices telling her that she was the Devil.

Davi noticed that something seemed wrong with her older brother Ed when he returned home from college for winter break. He seemed spaced out, and it looked as if he had not showered in several days. He carried a Bible with him everywhere. Several times she noticed Ed talking to himself when he thought that no one was around. Davi knew something was wrong, but she hoped it would go away.

It did not. Several months later, Davi's parents got a phone call from Ed's college. He had skipped all of his classes the past three weeks and had spent his time standing in front of a convenience store, reciting passages from the Bible. The previous week, the police had found Ed wandering around in the middle of a busy street. He seemed confused and disoriented, and when he spoke, his words were jumbled and hard to understand.

Many people, including figures on TV and the radio, know very little about schizophrenia. They often assume that having schizophrenia means having multiple personalities or being a dangerous maniac. This is not true. Schizophrenia is an illness, just like diabetes or heart disease. The only difference is that schizophrenia affects a person's mental health instead of his or her physical health.

Because the symptoms of schizophrenia can first appear during adolescence, it is important for teens to find out more about the illness. This book discusses what schizophrenia is, how it is diagnosed and treated, and what factors may play a role in causing it. By reading this book and others like it, you can begin to inform both yourself and others of the facts about schizophrenia. Understanding what schizophrenia is all about is the first step toward helping people to better cope with this illness.

Chapter One

What Is Schizophrenia?

Schizophrenia is a serious illness that affects the brain and causes major problems with thinking, emotions, and behavior. Many people with schizophrenia hear or see things that are not really there, have strange beliefs that other people do not share, or speak and behave in a disorganized way that is hard for other people to understand.

People with schizophrenia also may have an unusual way of showing emotions; for example, they may laugh at something that is actually very sad or may not change their facial expression very much at all. All people with schizophrenia do not necessarily have the same symptoms. In fact, symptoms can vary so widely that many people in the mental health field think of schizophrenia as a group of mental disorders rather than just one.

How Do You Know If Someone Has Schizophrenia?

People with schizophrenia often exhibit problems in many areas. Some of the most typical signs are delusions, hallucinations, disorganized speech, negative symptoms (such as blunted affect, poverty of speech, and avolition), and disorganized or catatonic behavior. Read on to find out more about these symptoms.

Delusions

Delusions are false beliefs that a person holds on to, despite the fact that there is strong evidence that the beliefs are wrong. People with delusions often believe that a person or a group of people is watching them and wants to hurt them.

Some people with schizophrenia may develop strange ideas about how the world works or may come to believe that they are famous or important people, such as Madonna or the president of the United States. They might believe that other people can read their mind or that someone is planting thoughts in, or stealing thoughts from, their brain.

Delusions are often based on real sensory experiences (experiences of the senses: vision, hearing, touch, taste, or smell) that are misinterpreted. To better understand how this misinterpretation happens, imagine walking into a restaurant. At the same moment that you walk in, a man sitting at the counter begins to cough. Most

Paranoid delusions can be a serious problem for people with schizophrenia.

people would not think twice about this coincidence and might not even notice it at all. A person who is suffering from delusions, however, may not only notice the cough, but may immediately decide that the man coughed to signal other people in the restaurant.

If, shortly after this incident, a woman eating in the restaurant makes a call on her cell phone, the person's delusion might become even more fixed. "Obviously the woman is calling someone to talk about me," the person thinks. If there is then a sudden power failure in the restaurant, the person thinks, "Obviously the woman on the cell phone was calling the power company to tell it to shut off the power in the restaurant." To the person suffering from delusions, everything seems to fit together.

Hallucinations

When a person hallucinates, he or she hears, sees, or feels something that is not really there. Many people with schizophrenia experience auditory hallucinations (hearing voices or noises that are not real). Sometimes people with auditory hallucinations hear voices that insult them or tell them what to do. Others might hear voices arguing with each other or might hear their own thoughts being spoken out loud.

Imagine what it would be like to hear voices twenty-four hours a day—voices that will not go away no matter what you do, even if you cover your ears or turn up your stereo really loud. One person with schizophrenia said that having auditory hallucinations is like listening to headphones with the volume on the highest level and not being able to turn it down in order to carry on conversations with people, read, watch TV, or even sleep.

Disorganized Speech

Another common symptom of schizophrenia is disorganized speech. Many people with schizophrenia have loose associations. This means that they leap from one idea to another even though the two ideas are not connected in any logical way. As a result, their speech is often very disorganized and hard for other people to understand.

Other people with disorganized speech may use made-up words that have meaning only to the person using them. Some may repeat the same words or state-ments over and over again. Still others may use rhyme as a guide to forming thoughts and statements.

Negative Symptoms

Negative symptoms are a group of schizophrenia symptoms that involve losses or deficits (a lower-than-normal amount of something) in certain areas. They include:

Blunted affect. Many people with schizophrenia have blunted affect, or trouble showing emo-tions. They show less anger, sadness, joy, and other feelings than most people do. They often have poor eye contact (they do not look at you when you speak to them) and their faces do not seem to change much when they interact with other people.

Poverty of speech. Some people with schizo-phrenia may think and say very little. Because of this, it might seem as if their thoughts are blocked. When asked questions, people with poverty of speech will often give short answers that do not carry much meaning.

Avolition. This refers to a symptom of schizo-phrenia that leads people to lose motivation to set goals for themselves and work toward these goals. These individuals may have trouble completing tasks at school, work, or home. Even things that seem easy to do may be very hard for a person who suffers from avolition.

Disorganized or Catatonic Behavior

The disorganized behavior of people with schizophrenia is often what leads others to feel afraid of them. Some people with schizophrenia might do bizarre things that are socially inappropriate, such as suddenly shouting or swearing in a public place. Others might show inappropriate affect, such as laughing uncontrollably at a relative's funeral or crying in situations that would usually make someone happy.

People with disorganized behavior often look dirty and disheveled, sometimes wearing light clothing on a cold day or a heavy winter coat and several sweaters on a warm day. People with schizophrenia often have a very hard time taking care of their basic needs, such as bathing, dressing properly, and even eating regularly.

Catatonia is a form of disorganized behavior that causes a person to become completely unaware of and unable to respond to the outside world. If left alone, some people with catatonia may sit motionless for hours. Sometimes a person with catatonia will place his or her body in an awkward, bizarre position (such as standing with arms straight out or balancing in a squatting pose) and will remain that way for hours

Schizophrenia can cause sufferers to show unusual behavior, such as dressing inappropriately for the weather.

without moving. Other times people with catatonia show the opposite symptoms, moving around excitedly and uncontrollably and wildly waving their arms or legs or repeating other unusual behaviors.

Chapter Two

Diagnosis and Development of Schizophrenia

There are many symptoms associated with schizophrenia, but people who have schizophrenia usually show only some of them. When a therapist is deciding whether to make a diagnosis of schizophrenia, he or she looks at a book called the *Diagnostic and Statistical Manual of Mental Disorders,* now in its fourth edition *(DSM-IV).*

The *DSM-IV* provides guidelines for how many symptoms the person must have and how severe the symptoms must be in order for the person to be diagnosed with the disorder. The *DSM-IV* calls for a diagnosis of schizophrenia when a person continuously shows two or more major symptoms of the disorder for at least six months. In addition, the person must show difficulties in one or more areas of functioning, such as work or school, relationships with others, and taking care of himself or herself (basic hygiene, grooming, etc.).

Schizophrenia Subtypes

Not all people with schizophrenia have the same symptoms. In fact, people with this illness often have very different groups of symptoms. For that reason, schizophrenia is subdivided into types, based on particular clusters (groups) of symptoms that often appear together. There are five subtypes of schizophrenia.

Subtype	Core Symptom(s)
1. Disorganized Type	Confusion, disorganized speech, and blunted or inappropriate affect
2. Catatonic Type	Catatonic behavior
3. Paranoid Type	Organized system of delusions and auditory hallucinations that often guide a person's behaviors
4. Residual Type	Symptoms of schizophrenia are lesser in intensity and number but are still present
5. Undifferentiated Type	Describes those who do not fall neatly into any of the other categories

Schizoaffective Disorder

Sometimes people have symptoms of a mood disorder in addition to symptoms of schizophrenia. A mood disorder is a disorder that affects a person's emotions. Major depression is a mood disorder that causes people to feel very sad and hopeless for long periods of time. People with major depression often have trouble sleeping, eat too much or too little, and lose interest in things that they usually enjoy. Another kind of mood disorder is bipolar disorder. People with bipolar disorder show symptoms of major depression at times, but at other times they become manic, meaning that they feel extremely happy (or, occasionally, irritable) and energetic. They feel so energetic that they go for long periods of time without sleeping and may often take risks and do things that they wouldn't ordinarily do, such as spend a lot of money on items that they cannot afford. When a person suffers from symptoms of a mood disorder along with symptoms of schizophrenia, they may receive a diagnosis of schizoaffective disorder.

How Common Is Schizophrenia?

Schizophrenia is not a rare illness. About one out of every one-hundred people in the world meets the *DSM-IV* criteria for schizophrenia. In the United States, it is estimated that more than two million people have been or will be diagnosed with the disorder at some point in their lifetime. This is larger than the total populations of seventeen states in the United States.

Schizophrenia affects men and women from every race, culture, and religion in just about every corner of the world. It also appears that schizophrenia may have been present throughout history. Some of the earliest known writings describe people with symptoms of a mental illness that sound very similar to the symptoms of schizophrenia.

How Does Schizophrenia Develop?

John was one of the brightest kids in his junior high school class and was a star player on the school basketball team.

By the time John reached high school, however, his family began to notice that something was wrong. John's grades dropped from As and Bs to Ds and Fs. He quit the basketball team because he believed that his teammates were spreading rumors about him. He began to spend most of his time in his room, refusing to speak to anyone.

John's family also noticed a change in his personality. He became quiet and withdrawn and often appeared to be spaced out when others tried to speak to him. John's parents began to worry that he might be using drugs.

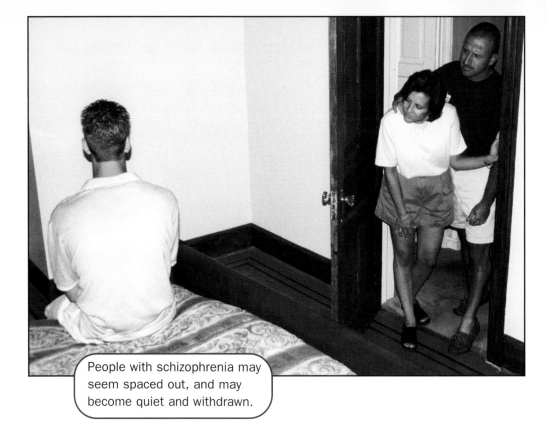

People with schizophrenia may seem spaced out, and may become quiet and withdrawn.

Families of individuals suffering from schizophrenia often report that recognizing the first signs of the disorder was very difficult. The first delusions and hallucinations are usually obvious signs of a serious problem, but there are usually more subtle signs and symptoms that occur even before these appear.

Some of these signs may include trouble concentrating, feelings of depression, sleeping more or less than usual, rapid weight loss, and withdrawal from friends and family. It is often difficult for family members and friends to tell whether these are signs of schizophrenia because these symptoms are common in other disorders, such as major depression. Some signs can also occur as a result of drug abuse or even just the normal stress associated with growing up.

The age at which the first symptoms of schizophrenia occur varies, but the illness most commonly strikes between the late teens and mid thirties. Although schizophrenia affects approximately equal numbers of men and women, men tend to be diagnosed at a younger age than women.

What Is the Course of Schizophrenia?

The course of schizophrenia (whether the person gets better or worse) varies tremendously between different people. Two individuals with the same symptoms at the onset of the illness may have completely different outcomes. Some people—about 25 percent of those with schizophrenia—respond very well to treatment and can return to the lives they led before. Most people with schizophrenia, however, continue to experience symptoms throughout their lifetime.

For many people with schizophrenia, the severity of their symptoms tends to fluctuate. Most people will experience times when the symptoms become worse as well as times when the symptoms are less intense. More information about treatments for schizophrenia, as well as about responses to treatment, is in chapters five and six.

Chapter Three

What Schizophrenia Is Not

The term "schizophrenia" has been used widely and often incorrectly in popular culture. In order to understand what schizophrenia is, it is also important to understand what schizophrenia is not.

Split or Multiple Personality Disorder

Schizophrenia is not the same thing as multiple or split personality even though many people mistakenly believe that it is. Multiple personality disorder, which is featured in books and movies like *Sybil* and *Dr. Jekyll and Mr. Hyde*, is referred to as dissociative identity disorder in the *DSM-IV*.

Dissociative identity disorder is a very rare mental illness in which two or more different personalities are present within the same person. Each of these personalities has his or her own memories, relationships, and ways of behaving, and only one of them is in charge at any one time. In contrast, people with schizophrenia have only one personality, although at times they may do things that they normally would not do.

Street Drug Psychosis

The abuse of street drugs such as LSD (acid), PCP (angel dust), or marijuana can produce symptoms that are similar to those of schizophrenia. When people take LSD or PCP, they often experience visual or auditory hallucinations. Marijuana use can cause delusions, especially the belief that people are watching the user and want to harm him or her. Unlike symptoms of schizophrenia, however, symptoms caused by street drugs almost always disappear within seventy-two hours after substance use has stopped.

Some people develop schizophrenia (and other mental disorders) around the same time that they begin using street drugs. For example, in the movie *The Wall*, it is not clear whether the main character's psychosis is caused by drug use, mental problems, or both.

For this reason, many relatives and friends of patients suffering from schizophrenia wonder whether the disorder was caused by drug abuse. Although street drugs can damage the brain and often produce symptoms that look like those of schizophrenia, it is very unlikely that the abuse of these drugs can actually cause schizophrenia in a person who is not already in the process of developing it.

A more likely explanation for the fact that some people develop schizophrenia around the same time they start using street drugs is that both of these things tend to happen at around the same age (teens to early twenties). Another explanation for the link between street-drug use and schizophrenia onset may be that people who are in the process of developing schizophrenia sometimes turn to mind-altering drugs to explain the frightening experiences they are having. Hearing voices for the first time in your life, for example, is a very frightening experience. If you then begin using marijuana or PCP, it provides you with a possible reason for hearing voices. You might reason that the voices are the result of the drugs rather than of a mental disorder that you cannot control.

Although there is currently no evidence that street-drug abuse causes schizophrenia, there is some evidence that it can make symptoms of schizophrenia worse. Also, schizophrenia researchers are still trying to find out if street-drug abuse can trigger schizophrenia in a person who is at risk for it. Risk factors for schizophrenia are discussed in chapter four.

Lifestyle Choice

Another false belief about schizophrenia, which was especially popular during the 1960s, is that people with schizophrenia are simply "marching to the beat of a different drummer." R. D. Laing, a Scottish psychiatrist, suggested that people choose to have schizophrenia and that schizophrenia is actually a process through which people try to cure themselves of confusion and unhappiness caused by family problems.

Laing thought that people with schizophrenia should not be given treatment to reduce their symptoms. He believed that if they were simply allowed to go through this process, they would become stronger and less confused. There is no evidence to support this theory, and most schizophrenia researchers today do not take this point of view.

What Is a Schizophrenic?

A common pop culture term for someone who suffers from schizophrenia is "schizophrenic." This word, however, overlooks the fact that people who suffer from schizophrenia are individuals with many qualities that have nothing to do with their illness.

When you call someone a schizophrenic, you are defining that person by his or her illness. The same is true for terms like "manic depressives," "borderlines," or "diabetics" when they are used to describe people with manic depressive disorder, borderline personality disorder, or diabetes, respectively. It is important to remember that a person may have a disorder, but he or she also has unique characteristics, skills, and experiences. Disorders, not people, should be classified.

The Wall depicts the world through the lens of psychosis.

Chapter Four

What Are the Causes of Schizophrenia?

Schizophrenia is a complicated disorder, and experts still do not know exactly what causes it. Over the years, people have come up with many theories (possible explanations) for the causes of schizophrenia. As researchers have learned more about the disorder, some of these theories have been rejected and others have been developed. Currently most people in the mental health field think that schizophrenia may be caused by a combination of factors.

Genetics

Genes are tiny parts of cells that carry traits (an individual's personal characteristics) from parents to children. They are like a "recipe" for a new person. People inherit genes from their parents, and traits that are controlled by genes are called inherited traits.

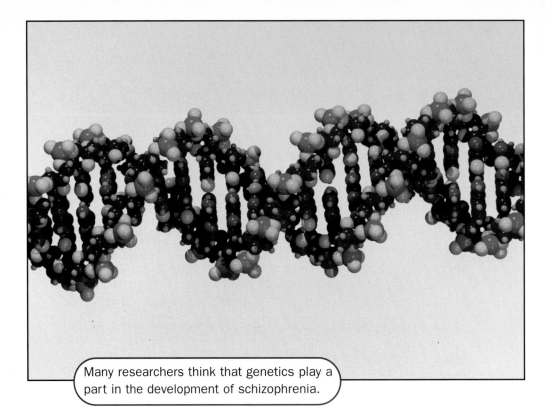

Many researchers think that genetics play a part in the development of schizophrenia.

For example, the color of your eyes is determined by your genes and is, therefore, said to be inherited. Many researchers believe that schizophrenia might be caused, at least partly, by inherited genes that increase a person's risk for developing the disorder.

Studies have shown that schizophrenia runs in families. That is, relatives of schizophrenia sufferers are more likely to develop the condition than people from families that are free of schizophrenia. Furthermore, closely related relatives, who share more of the same genes with the schizophrenia sufferer than do more distant relatives, are even more likely to develop the disorder.

Identical vs. Fraternal Twins

Identical twins share all of the same genes, whereas fraternal (nonidentical) twins share only about half of the same genes. This fact has allowed scientists to find out important information about the role of genes in causing schizophrenia.

Studies show that a person whose identical twin has schizophrenia is much more likely to develop schizophrenia than a person whose nonidentical twin has schizophrenia. The risk for schizophrenia for the identical twin is about 40 to 60 percent, and the risk for the nonidentical twin is about 20 percent. This means that the more genes a person shares with a schizophrenia sufferer, the greater his or her risk is for developing schizophrenia. The risk for more distant relatives, such as grandchildren or nieces and nephews of people with schizophrenia, is less than 10 percent.

How Do Genes Cause Schizophrenia?

Schizophrenia researchers have two major theories about the way that genes play a role in causing schizophrenia. Both theories assume that inherited genes cause the brain of a person with schizophrenia to develop in an abnormal way. According to one theory, the person develops an abnormal brain structure, meaning that the shape and size of certain parts of the brain may be different from those in a normal brain.

The other theory suggests that the activity of certain chemicals in the brain, called neurotransmitters, may be abnormal. Neurotransmitters carry messages to different parts of the body. They play an important role in emotions, movement, learning, and memory.

Brain Structure and Activity

Scientists have developed several techniques for taking pictures of the brain. One of these techniques, called MRI (magnetic resonance imaging), uses magnetic fields and radio waves to produce pictures of the brain. Another technique is called PET (positron emission tomography). This technique uses radiation to measure how much activity is occurring in certain parts of the brain.

Studies using MRI and PET have found differences between the brains of people who have schizophrenia and people who do not. Researchers have reported that certain structures in the brain may be smaller in schizophrenia sufferers and that the spaces between structures (called ventricles) may be larger. Also, studies using PET have found that certain parts of the brain are less active in people with schizophrenia than in healthy people.

The story is not so simple, however. Brain structure abnormalities have not been found in all individuals with schizophrenia (that is, there are people with schizophrenia whose brains appear to have the same structure as that of a healthy person). In addition, some similar brain abnormalities have been found in patients who are

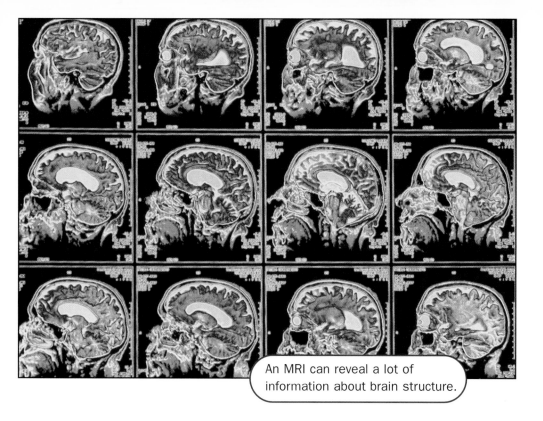

An MRI can reveal a lot of information about brain structure.

not suffering from schizophrenia but have other disorders, such as bipolar disorder and Alzheimer's disease.

Some studies suggest that certain differences in brain structure and activity might be linked with specific schizophrenia symptoms. For example, people who have disorganized speech are likely to have abnormalities in one area of the brain, and people who have mostly negative symptoms are likely to have abnormalities in another.

This type of research is still relatively new. As technology improves and machines that produce clearer pictures of the brain and its functioning are developed, it is likely that the role of brain abnormalities in schizophrenia will become clearer.

Neurotransmitters

Schizophrenia researchers believe that at least some of the symptoms of schizophrenia may be caused by having too much of a neurotransmitter called dopamine in the brain. Several observations led to this theory. First, drugs called amphetamines, which cause a rise in dopamine levels in the brain, can cause a person to have symptoms that look like those of schizophrenia. Second, if a person who suffers from schizophrenia takes a drug that increases dopamine levels in the brain, his or her symptoms often become worse. Third, it is now known that drugs that are helpful in reducing schizophrenia symptoms block dopamine action. See chapter five for more information about drug treatments for schizophrenia and how they work.

Environment

Genes play an important role in causing schizophrenia, but they do not cause schizophrenia all by themselves. For this reason, many schizophrenia researchers believe that schizophrenia itself is not inherited, but rather only a risk for the disorder is inherited. They believe that people who have inherited a risk for schizophrenia will develop the disorder only if they are exposed to an environmental stressor (an event or condition in a person's surroundings that triggers an illness).

This theory is similar to that for other medical diseases, such as heart disease. For example, a person might inherit a risk for heart disease because he or she has a parent with heart problems. However, the person may or may not develop heart problems, depending on several environmental factors, such as the person's eating and exercise habits as well as the amount of daily stress he or she experiences.

Schizophrenia researchers are still working to find out what kinds of environmental stressors may combine with a genetic risk to cause schizophrenia. This mechanism would be similar to the way that an unhealthy diet can combine with a genetic risk to cause heart disease.

Biological Environmental Stressors

Several biological stressors have been studied as possible partial causes of schizophrenia. Several studies suggest that mothers of people with schizophrenia may have been exposed to a biological stressor while they were pregnant.

For example, severe outbreaks of the flu, such as the one that occurred in England in 1958, have been associated with an increase in the rate of schizophrenia twenty to thirty years later. It is possible that an unusually large number of unborn children were exposed to the flu virus during this time and that this exposure caused their brains to develop abnormally.

Some of these children may have also inherited a risk for schizophrenia. The genetic risk, combined with exposure to the flu virus, may have caused schizophrenia symptoms to be expressed when the child reached adulthood. Studies also reveal an increased rate of schizophrenia in people born during the spring and winter months in areas of the world with cold winters. Babies born during those seasons are more likely to have been exposed to the flu while in their mother's womb because there is a higher rate of the flu during the winter months.

Another early environmental stressor that may combine with a genetic risk to cause schizophrenia is a complication during the birth process. Researchers have found that people with schizophrenia are more likely to have suffered from birth complications (such as not getting enough oxygen during delivery) than people who do not have schizophrenia. Most babies born under these conditions, however, do not develop schizophrenia. It is likely that birth complications cause schizophrenia only if the person is also genetically at risk for the disorder.

Family Stress

At one time, many mental health professionals believed that schizophrenia was caused by family problems. In particular, many people believed that schizophrenia resulted from having a cold and unloving mother. The term "schizophrenogenic mother" was made up to describe these mothers who supposedly caused schizophrenia. There is no scientific evidence to support this theory. Having a mean and unloving family does not cause schizophrenia.

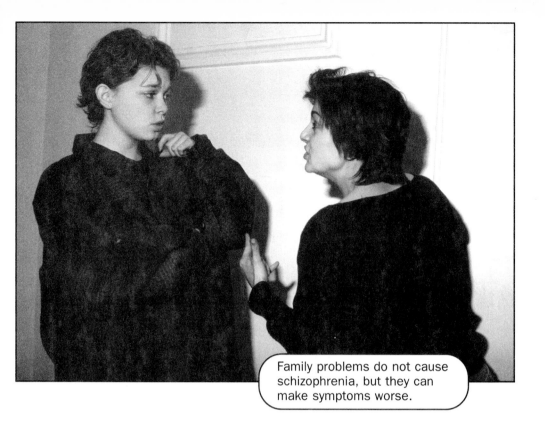

Family problems do not cause schizophrenia, but they can make symptoms worse.

However, even though family stress clearly does not cause schizophrenia, some studies suggest that inter-actions with family members may affect the course of schizophrenia once a person has already developed the illness. As mentioned in chapter two, people who suffer from schizophrenia usually go through periods when their symptoms are better and other periods when their symptoms are worse. Symptoms can become so serious that the person has to go to the hospital. Some studies have shown that schizophrenia sufferers whose families are hostile and criticize them may be more likely to be hospitalized and to experi-ence more periods of worsened symptoms.

Chapter Five

Medical Treatments for Schizophrenia

Schizophrenia is a treatable disease. This does not mean that schizophrenia is curable, however. To say that schizophrenia is treatable means that its symptoms can be controlled. In contrast, saying that there is a cure for schizophrenia would mean that a permanent removal of all of its causes is possible. Curing schizophrenia will not become possible until we truly understand its causes. In the meantime, schizophrenia researchers are working to improve treatments for this disorder.

Antipsychotics (Neuroleptics)

Without question, the most important development in the treatment of schizophrenia symptoms occurred in the 1950s, when antipsychotic medications were first discovered to reduce the symptoms of schizophrenia. Antipsychotic medications are also called neuroleptics because, in addition to their helpful effects, these medications often have side effects that are similar to the symptoms of some neurological (brain) disorders, such as Parkinson's disease. More information about side effects is given later in this chapter.

Neuroleptic medications were not originally developed to treat schizophrenia. It was not until the 1950s that a neuroleptic medication called chlorpromazine was first discovered to be very effective for calming schizophrenia sufferers. People in the mental health field now believe that neuroleptic medications work because they block the action of dopamine in the brain (see chapter four).

Research shows that neuroleptic medications reduce schizophrenia symptoms in about two-thirds of patients. For about one-third of people with schizophrenia, neuroleptics control their symptoms almost completely. For another third, the drugs work to reduce the symptoms but do not make them go away entirely. The remaining third suffer from severe symptoms that cannot be controlled by neuroleptic medications.

Neuroleptic medications work especially well for treating hallucinations and also help control delusions and disorganized speech. These medications do not work very well for treating negative symptoms, such as blunted affect, poverty of speech, and avolition.

Antipsychotic Drugs

Antipsychotic drugs vary in how long they take to work. Also, they work faster in some people than in others. Some individuals experience a dramatic improvement within two days of starting medication. For others, improvement takes several weeks.

Individuals also vary in how long they need to continue taking medication. Some people—about one quarter—recover completely after only one episode of schizophrenia. These people may be able to stop taking antipsychotic medication within a few weeks following their recovery. However, most people who stop taking antipsychotic medications experience a relapse, or return of symptoms. The treatment of schizophrenia can be compared to the treatment of diabetes. People who have diabetes take insulin to manage their symptoms, not to get rid of the causes of the illness. The insulin controls diabetes, but it does not cure it.

Like diabetes, there is no cure for schizophrenia; there are only medications to control its symptoms. Therefore, most people who take antipsychotic drugs to control schizophrenia symptoms need to remain on these medications for a long time, often for several years.

Negative Side Effects of Neuroleptics

Unfortunately, in addition to the positive effects of antipsychotic drugs (the reduction of schizophrenia symptoms), these medications sometimes produce unwanted side effects. Many people who take neuroleptics report that the medications make them feel "slowed down" and groggy. These medications can also cause dryness of the mouth, blurred vision, and weight gain.

Neuroleptics can also lead to disturbing movement problems, which are called extrapyramidal side effects (EPS). EPS resemble the symptoms of a neurological disease called Parkinson's disease. People with EPS often feel their muscles become very stiff. Typically, they shuffle their feet when they walk, and their hands shake or tremble.

Another kind of EPS leads a person to lose control of some of his or her movements. For example, people with this side effect might smack their lips or make chewing motions that they cannot control. This syndrome, which usually occurs in patients who have taken neuroleptics for at least several years, is known as tardive dyskinesia.

People who have tardive dyskinesia move their tongue and mouth uncontrollably. They often make involuntary jerking movements, such as chewing, sucking, smacking their lips, or pushing their cheeks out with their tongues. Sometimes they lose control over muscles in other parts of the body and make unusual jerky movements with their arms or legs.

Reducing the amount of medication the person is taking or having him or her switch to a different medication usually reduces the severity of tardive dyskinesia. Also, there are newer medical treatments for schizophrenia, discussed later, that do not seem to cause tardive dyskinesia.

Most people with schizophrenia who take neuroleptic medications do not experience severe side effects. Most people who do experience side effects report that the side effects are not as bad as the hallucinations, delusions, and disorganization that the medications control.

Some schizophrenia sufferers, however, stop taking their medication because of the side effects or because they feel that they do not need medication anymore when their symptoms go away. Unfortunately, most of these people will suffer a relapse of symptoms within a few months of stopping their medication.

New Antipsychotics

In recent years, researchers have developed several new antipsychotic drugs that can be given to schizophrenia sufferers who experience severe side effects from or who do not respond to neuroleptic medications. These new medications are called atypical antipsychotics because they work in a different way from, and have a different effect than, traditional neuroleptics. Scientists are not yet completely sure how these medications work, but the substances seem to affect the action of other neurotransmitters in the brain in addition to dopamine.

A rare side effect of clozapine is a dangerous drop in the body's white blood cells count.

The most effective and widely used atypical antipsychotic drug is called clozapine. Clozapine has been found to work for nearly 85 percent of patients with schizophrenia. Unlike traditional neuroleptics, it helps to relieve negative symptoms in addition to positive symptoms. Also, clozapine appears to cause fewer extrapyramidal side effects than do the older antipsychotic medications, and there have been few, if any, cases of tardive dyskinesia that have resulted from clozapine use.

Unfortunately, clozapine can have a serious side effect of its own. People who use this drug have a 1 to 2 percent risk of developing a condition called agranulocytosis. This condition can be life-threatening because it causes a drop in the number of white blood cells in the body. A loss of white blood cells is dangerous because they are the body's main line of defense for fighting infections. Therefore, people who take clozapine have to monitor their white blood cell count each week. If a blood test reveals a drop in the number of white blood cells, use of clozapine is immediately stopped.

There are other atypical antipsychotic medications that have been recently developed, such as risperidone and olanzapine, that do not cause agranulocytosis.

Chapter Six

Psychological Treatments for Schizophrenia

When Molly first got home from the hospital, she felt great. The medication was finally working, and the angry voices in her head shouting at her and telling her to hurt herself were gone. She no longer believed that her room was bugged with microphones and that spies were trying to steal her thoughts. She was beginning to feel like her old self again, and she was ready to go back to her old life.

However, Molly quickly realized that returning to her old life would not be as easy as she had thought. The antipsychotic medication that she was taking frequently made her feel sleepy, and she had also begun to gain weight. When Molly called up her old friends from high school, she realized that they had moved on with their lives while she had been in the hospital.

Her best friend, Bernice, had gone off to college and now had a new social life that did not include Molly. Also, Molly noticed that Bernice seemed awkward when they talked on the phone—as if she was afraid that Molly would begin talking about spies again or something. As for Molly's parents, well, they seemed to be walking on eggshells around her, as if they were afraid that she could "snap" at any time.

Picking Up the Pieces

Although antipsychotic medications can be very successful in controlling symptoms of schizophrenia, there are many aspects of the disorder that medications do not help. Once the intense hallucinations, delusions, or other major symptoms of the disorder are controlled, schizophrenia sufferers are left to pick up the pieces of the life they left behind.

It is at this point that many schizophrenia sufferers begin to realize that even if the medications control the symptoms completely, their lives will be forever changed by schizophrenia. Many people who are recovering from schizophrenia report that they have a lot of trouble relating to family members and friends. Also, they may realize that goals they had set before their illness (such as being accepted to a competitive college or getting a high-powered job) may now be too difficult to achieve.

In addition, people who are recovering from the symptoms of schizophrenia often complain about the side effects of medications. Many resent having to stay on these medications even though their symptoms have gone away. A type of treatment that helps schizophrenia sufferers deal with the huge psychological impact of schizophrenia is called psychotherapy.

Psychotherapy

Psychotherapy is a type of treatment in which a mental health professional (psychiatrist, psychologist, or social worker) uses words and sometimes activities to help a person overcome psychological difficulties.

Before the discovery of antipsychotic drugs, psychotherapy by itself was not really helpful for people with schizophrenia. Most patients were just too far removed from reality to benefit from psychotherapy. Today, however, psychotherapy is an important part of treatment for many people with schizophrenia.

Medications help to relieve symptoms such as hallucinations, delusions, and disorganized speech. Psychotherapy helps patients to play an active role in the treatment process, think more clearly about themselves and their relationships, and make positive changes in their behavior. Three kinds of psychotherapy that are often helpful for treating people with schizophrenia are individual therapy, group therapy, and family therapy.

Individual Therapy

Individual therapy refers to psychotherapy in which the patient meets one-on-one with a therapist. There are many different kinds of individual therapy. Some individual therapists simply provide a safe place for patients with schizophrenia to talk about difficulties associated with their illness and to receive support. Other individual therapists may play a more active role in the therapy, providing advice and training in areas in which the patient needs help.

For example, a therapist might give Molly some suggestions about how to deal with the awkwardness that she feels around her parents. He or she may also explore with Molly the best way for her to express her feelings to her parents in a positive and helpful way.

Group Therapy

Many people with schizophrenia find it helpful to participate in group therapy. Group therapy usually consists of one or two therapists who work with a group of patients who share similar problems. Groups usually involve some sort of training for the patients in areas that create problems for them.

For example, many people with schizophrenia find it difficult to make friends. There are several reasons for this. First, some of the negative symptoms of the illness, such as poor eye contact and difficulty showing emotions, may interfere with social interactions. (Next time you see your best friend, try maintaining a flat expression and looking at the floor while you talk to him or her. It probably will not be long until your friend becomes very uncomfortable and asks you what is wrong!)

Also, some people with schizophrenia have trouble deciding how to appropriately initiate (start off) contact with other people. In addition, many schizophrenia sufferers have trouble dealing with the stigma (shame or disgrace) of being known as a mentally ill person. This stigma may cause a person to be rejected by old friends or others who are not mentally ill. Some schizophrenia sufferers may reject others who suffer from mental illness because they feel ashamed of their own illness and do not want to be around other "sick" people.

Therefore, one type of group therapy might focus on helping people with schizophrenia learn to act appropriately in social situations and make friends. The therapist running the group might do this by having two people in the group act out a social situation:

> **Therapist:** *OK, we're going to practice talking to someone with the goal of getting to know the person a little better. Darius, why don't you try it first with Janice. Pretend that she is standing by a bus stop and that you're both waiting to take the same bus. You want to try to talk to her a little.*
> **Darius:** *Okay. Hi, do you want to go to the movies?*

Group therapy can be very helpful in treating schizophrenia.

Janice: Well, I don't really know you.

Therapist: Start a little more slowly, Darius. Try to let Janice know that you know who she is and that you'd like to introduce yourself.

Darius: Hi, my name is Darius. I've seen you waiting for this bus before.

Janice: Yes, I take this bus three days a week.

Therapist: That's a big improvement, Darius. Janice, if someone introduces himself, you should respond by telling him your name. Let's start again with Darius.

Darius: Hi, my name is Darius. I think I've seen you here before.

Janice: Yes, I take this bus three days a week. My name is Janice.

Therapist: Great job. That's much better. Janice, you might then ask Darius how often he takes the bus so that you'll have something more to talk about. Also, Darius, try to look at Janice when you talk to her instead of looking down at your feet.

Group therapy also provides an opportunity for people with schizophrenia to meet other people who are in a similar situation. They can often provide support and advice for each other. Group therapy often results in the formation of strong and lasting friendships.

Family Therapy

Approximately 65 percent of individuals with schizophrenia live with family members. This can create special pressures for both patients and their family members. As mentioned in chapter four, family stress does not cause schizophrenia. However, interactions with family members can affect whether a person experiences a relapse (return of symptoms) once his or her symptoms have been controlled with medication.

The most common cause of relapse is when a patient stops taking medication. However, a relapse can sometimes occur even when the person takes his or her medication faithfully. One factor that may increase the risk of relapse is living with family members who are critical of and hostile to the person with schizophrenia or who are smothering and overinvolved in the person's life.

One of the goals of family therapy is to help families learn to interact with their relative in a way that reduces his or her risk of relapse. Family therapy also provides an opportunity for all family members to learn more about schizophrenia. For example, family members often do not know much about the negative symptoms of the illness and may sometimes confuse them with laziness. In addition, family therapy provides support and guidance for family members who are worried about their relative.

Getting Help

A few weeks after returning home from the hospital, Molly began seeing Dr. Kitay, a psychologist who specializes in working with people recovering from schizophrenia. Molly told Dr. Kitay about the difficulties she was having with her family and her old friends. She also expressed her frustration with taking a medication that caused her to feel sleepy and gain weight.

Dr. Kitay helped Molly to realize how important her medication was and that the side effects were not nearly as bad as having to go to the hospital again. Dr. Kitay also helped Molly to understand why relating to her parents seemed so difficult. Dr. Kitay even met with Molly's parents several times to help them learn more about her illness.

In addition, Dr. Kitay encouraged Molly to participate in a support group with other young people recovering from schizophrenia. Molly resisted at first because she wanted to leave her illness behind her instead of hanging out with other "sick" people. However, after a few sessions, Molly discovered that she really enjoyed group therapy. She found it helpful to talk about her problems with other people in similar situations. Molly also realized that she was able to help others in the group to feel better, just as they were able to help her.

Chapter Seven | When Someone You Love Has Schizophrenia

"**M**y sister Jess was diagnosed with schizophrenia only a few months ago," Sarah says. "I've tried to understand what she's going through, but it's really hard. I'm only thirteen.

"I wish things could be like they were before. Jess used to laugh at my jokes and smile all the time. Now she just seems to stare off into space with no expression on her face, or she laughs and talks to herself when she thinks no one's looking.

"I live in a small town, and people don't seem to know much about schizophrenia here. People make jokes a lot about 'psychos' or say dumb things like, 'My name is Bob and I'm schizophrenic—no wait, I'm Fred—no, Bob.'

"My family has kept Jess's problem a secret so far. When people ask me what's wrong with her,

Schizophrenia can affect financial matters in the family.

I tell them she's just depressed. I feel bad lying, but it's so much easier than telling people she has schizophrenia.

"My parents are going through hell, too. My mother keeps blaming herself for not being a better parent. My dad tries to pretend that nothing's wrong and keeps saying that Jess would get better if she would just get off her butt and get a job. They also worry about money a lot because the doctor bills are so expensive.

"I feel so alone. When I come home from school, my parents never ask how my day was. They talk only about Jess and how the medicine hasn't been working. I just want all this to end."

Schizophrenia and Your Family

Schizophrenia affects the whole family. It can be especially tough for brothers and sisters of schizophrenia sufferers. If you are a brother or sister of someone with schizophrenia, you may be feeling many of the following emotions:

Guilt. Healthy siblings often feel guilty about not being the sick one. Sometimes the healthy sibling may feel the need to be supersuccessful in order to make up for the ill sibling's failures and avoid causing more problems for the parents.

Resentment. It is not at all unusual for healthy siblings to feel occasional resentment toward the ill sibling. Often parents spend so much time worrying about their child with schizophrenia that they do not save enough time and attention for their healthy children.

Grief. Healthy siblings may often feel grief over the loss of their relationship with their brother or sister—the way it "used to be."

Worry. Because schizophrenia seems to be at least partly inherited, many siblings of people with schizophrenia worry that they might also become sick one day.

Embarrassment. Because of the stigma and embarrassment surrounding mental illness, families often try to hide the illness from others. This can be especially tough for siblings. It is already hard enough for kids and teenagers to feel as though they fit in. The last thing they want people to think is that their brother or sister is "psycho." This can result in feelings of loneliness because they feel that they have no one to talk to. To make things worse, people generally know very little about schizophrenia and may tell jokes or make comments that spread inaccurate information about the illness. For example, in Sarah's town, people make jokes about someone with schizophrenia having multiple personalities; as you know from reading this book, however, schizophrenia is actually very different from multiple personality disorder.

Confusion. When a loved one becomes sick, it is natural to try to find an explanation for the illness. Even though it is well established that schizophrenia, much like heart disease or diabetes, has a biological cause, many people find themselves wondering if they did something to cause the illness: "What if I had paid more attention to him when he was younger?" "Maybe I shouldn't have expected her to do so much." Although we do not yet know the exact causes of schizophrenia, we do know that people do not cause the illness by being mean or demanding any more than a person can cause diabetes or cancer in this way.

Sources for Help

If someone you care about has schizophrenia, you may feel that there is no one to talk to who understands what you are going through. There are people and organizations that can offer support and advice, however. Reading about schizophrenia and speaking with other people who are in a situation similar to your own are good ways to start helping yourself feel less alone.

One good source of support is the National Alliance for the Mentally Ill (NAMI), a national organization for people coping with mental illness in their families. NAMI can help you get in touch with other young people who are struggling with schizophrenia or other mental illnesses in their families.

Another valuable resource for learning more about dealing with schizophrenia in the family is the World Wide Web. There are Internet chat rooms and message boards especially for siblings or other family members of people with schizophrenia. Some helpful phone numbers and Web sites are listed in the back of this book.

Glossary

bipolar disorder Mood disorder that causes extreme mood swings. The person feels very sad and hopeless at certain times and extremely happy (or occasionally irritable) and energetic at other times.

blunted affect A symptom of schizophrenia that is characterized by a person displaying less emotion— anger, sadness, joy—than most other people.

dissociative identity disorder Very rare mental illness in which two or more distinct personalities are present within the same person. Each of these personalities has his or her own memories, relationships, and ways of behaving, and only one of them is in charge at any given moment.

dopamine A kind of neurotransmitter (chemical messenger) that researchers think may play a role in causing symptoms of schizophrenia.

extrapyramidal side effects (EPS) Side effects of neuroleptics that can cause a person's muscles to become stiff, their hands to shake, and their feet to shuffle when they walk. EPS can also cause a person's facial muscles to move uncontrollably.

genes Tiny parts of cells that carry traits from parents to children and are like a "recipe" for a new person.

inappropriate affect A symptom of schizophrenia characterized by a person expressing emotions that do not fit the situation.

inherited traits Traits that are determined by genes.

mood disorder Disorder affecting a person's emotional state; includes major depression and bipolar disorder.

negative symptoms Symptoms of schizophrenia that reflect deficits or characteristics that seem to be lacking. They include blunted affect, poverty of speech, and avolition.

neurotransmitters Chemicals in the brain that carry messages to different parts of the body and play an important role in emotions, movement, learning, and memory.

poverty of speech A symptom of schizophrenia characterized by a reduced amount of talking.

psychotherapy Type of treatment in which a mental health professional uses words and sometimes activities to help a person overcome psychological difficulties.

Where to Go for Help

In the United States

American Family Therapy Association
2020 Pennsylvania Avenue, NW
Washington, DC 20005
(202) 994-2776

American Psychological Association
750 First Street, NE
Washington, DC 20002
(202) 336-5500
Web site: http://www.apa.com

American Psychological Society
1010 Vermont Avenue, NW, Suite 1100
Washington, DC 20005-4907
(202) 783-2077
Web site: http://www.aps.com

National Alliance for the Mentally Ill (NAMI)
200 North Glebe Road, Suite 1015
Arlington, VA 22203-3754
(800) 950-NAMI
Web site: http://www.aamff.org

National Alliance for Research on Schizophrenia and
    Depression
208 South LaSalle Street
Chicago, IL 60604
(312) 641-1666

National Mental Health Association
1021 Prince Street
Alexandria, VA 22314-2971
(800) 969-NMHA
Web site: http://www.nmha.org

National Mental Health Consumer Self-Help
    Clearinghouse
311 South Juniper Street
Philadelphia, PA 19107
(215) 735-6367

Schizophrenics Anonymous
15920 West Twelve Mile
Southfield, MI 48076
(313) 477-1983

Youth Crisis Hotline
(800) 448-4663

In Canada

Canadian Mental Health Association
2610 Yonge Street
Toronto, ON M4S 2Z3
(416) 484-7750

Canadian Schizophrenic Foundation
P.O. Box 35331, Station E
Vancouver, BC V6M 3C8

Schizophrenia Society of Canada
814-75 The Donway West
North York, ON M3C 3E9
(416) 445-8204

Web Sites

Facts for Families Schizophrenia in Children
http://www.aacap.org/web/aacap/factsFam

National Institute of Mental Health
    Schizophrenia Q & A
http://www.nimh.nih.gov/publist/specific.htm

Schizophrenia Home Page
http://www.schizophrenia.com

Schizophrenia Newsgroup
http://www.alt.support.schizophrenia

Schizophrenia Support Organizations
http://www.members.aol.com/leonardjk/support.htm

For Further Reading

Dinner, Sherry. *Nothing to Be Ashamed Of: Growing Up with Mental Illness in Your Family.* New York: William Morrow, 1989.

Foster, Constance. *Out of the Jungle: A Survival Guide with Compass.* Ellsworth, ME: Dilligaf Publishing, 1994.

Hoffer, Abram, et al. *How to Live with Schizophrenia.* Secaucus, NJ: Carol Publishing, 1997.

Hyland, Betty. *The Girl with the Crazy Brother.* New York: Franklin Watts, 1987.

Jeffries, J.J., et al. *Living and Working with Schizophrenia.* Buffalo, NY: University of Toronto Press, 1990.

Johnson, Julie. *Understanding Mental Illness for Teens Who Care About Someone with Mental Illness.* Minneapolis, MN: Lerner Publishing, 1989.

Mueser, Kim T. *Coping with Schizophrenia: A Guide for Families.* Oakland, CA: New Harbinger Publications, 1994.

Index

About the Author

Michelle Friedman has worked extensively at the New York State Psychiatric Institute and the Brockton VA Medical Center with schizophrenia sufferers. Currently, she is pursuing a doctoral degree in clinical psychology at the University of Massachusetts–Boston and conducts research on the neuropsychology of schizophrenia. This is her first book.

Photo Credits

Cover and pp. 2, 6, 11, 15, 20, 48, 53 by Kristen Artz; pp. 28, 41 © Custom Medical; p. 31 © FPG; p. 26 © The Everett Collection; p. 35 by John Novejosky.

Layout Design

Michael J. Caroleo